SNAKES: 101 SUPER FUN FACTS AND AMAZING PICTURES

(FEATURING THE WORLD's TOP 10 SNAKES)

Table of Contents

Are you afraid of snakes?

Many people find snakes creepy and frightening. It's a normal reaction, since snakes are strange creatures that don't look so friendly and cuddly. People are also scared to get bitten by snakes because they have poisonous fangs.

However, snakes are mostly misunderstood creatures. There are different circumstances which explain why a snake usually attacks humans. You probably would not one as a pet at home, but you would definitely understand them better with these fascinating facts scientists have discovered about snakes in general.

Figure 1: Not all snakes are dangerous to humans. These kids are playing with harmless varieties of snakes.

Snake Facts

1. Snakes are reptiles, cold-blooded creatures or creatures that adjust body temperatures according to their environment. They belong to the sub-order serpentia, a group of flexible, long and crawling reptiles.

2. There are almost 3,000 known species of snakes worldwide, but only 375 are venomous. They are found everywhere except in extremely cold places like Antarctica, Iceland, and Greenland.

3. Snakes have noses, but they use their tongues to smell things. This is why snakes often stick their tongues out, creating the hissing sound we hear from them.

4. Snakes kill their prey either by injecting venom through their fangs or by choking them by wrapping their bodies around them.

5. Snakes are deaf and have poor eyesight, but their sense of smell is strong. They can also feel sound vibrations.

Figure 2: All snakes have teeth, but only poisonous snakes have fangs. They use these fangs to inject poison on their prey.

6. Snakes regulate their body temperature by sunning themselves or moving to cooler places. During the winter, snakes often go to long periods of sleep called hibernation.

7. Snakes swallow their prey whole. A snake's throat stretches to accommodate the size of its prey, and its stomach contains the necessary substances to digest them.

8. Snakes take a long time digesting their prey. In fact, some species may live without eating again for as long as one year!

9. Like lizards, snakes shed their skins regularly as they grow bigger. They do this by rubbing their bodies on rough surfaces, such as a rock. Snakes shed around 3 to 6 times yearly.

10. Most snakes reproduce by laying eggs. Only a few species can hatch baby snakes directly from their bodies.

Figure 3: Snakes shed their old skin because they no longer fit in them. Shedding also removes unwanted parasites living in their old skin.

11. In captivity, some snakes have been recorded to live for as long as 50 years. Their life span in the wild has not yet been determined.

12.　　　Snakes are nocturnal. They are more active at night than during the day.

13.　　　Female snakes produce hormones called pheromones when they are ready to mate. This leaves a scent trail to be followed by male snakes. The mating process lasts at least an hour, and could even last the whole day.

14.　　　Their skin coloring and markings often act as camouflage against their predators. Aside from humans, snakes have a lot of enemies, including birds of prey, raccoons, bears, and foxes.

Figure 4: Snakes often choose to lay their eggs underground in order to incubate them. Most snakes abandon their eggs immediately after laying them.

Figure 5: snake: A male and female snake mates with each other to produce their young. The mating season lasts several months before the eggs or baby snakes are born.

The World's Top 10 Snakes

Of all snake species, the following species are the most fascinating ones. Many of these snakes have often been the subject of horror movies and myths.

- Anaconda
- Boa Constrictor
- Cobra
- Corn Snake
- Garter Snake
- Python
- Rattlesnake
- Sea Snake
- California King Snake
- Milk Snake

The following are just some amazing facts about these snake breeds that scientists have been able to discover.

Anaconda (Eunectes murinus)

Figure 6: An anaconda opens its jaws wide to attack its prey. Its jaws are not hinged, so they can stretch wide enough to swallow prey larger than the anaconda's diameter.

Scientific classification

1. Kingdom:	Animalia
2. Phylum:	Chordata
3. Subphylum:	Vertebrata
4. Class:	Reptilia
5. Order:	Squamata
6. Suborder:	Serpentes
7. Family:	Boidae
8. Genus:	Eunectes
9. Species:	E. murinus

15.   The anaconda, also known as the green anaconda, is the heaviest snake in the world. They can reach a body length of up to 16 feet and weigh 70 to 150 lbs.!

16.   Anacondas are not poisonous. They kill their prey by wrapping their massive bodies around it and squeezing until the prey is dead.

17.   Anacondas are a species of boa snakes primarily found in South American rain forests. They are distinguishable by their olive green skin peppered with black blotch-like marks. Their eyes are located at the top of their heads.

18.   A group of anacondas is called a knot.

19.   Anacondas love to swim. They can submerge themselves fully underwater and wait for their prey to approach.

20.   Anacondas feed not only on birds and fishes, but also on larger animals like tapirs, wild pigs, capybaras and occasionally jaguars. Some have even been reported to eat fellow anacondas.

21.   Anacondas are solitary creatures. They only mingle during "breeding balls," a gathering of anacondas for the sole purpose of mating.

22.   Anaconda eggs are hatched within their mother's body. A female anaconda can give birth to as much as 80 baby anacondas at once. Each baby snake can reach up to 2 feet long.

23.   Humans pose the biggest threat to anacondas. Not only do humans kill anacondas out of fear, their skin is also sold illegally in different parts around the world.

Boa Constrictor (Boa constrictor constrictor)

Figure 7: As their name indicates, boa constrictors kill their prey through constriction. Their teeth are designed not to break down food, but only to hook their prey while they strangle them.

Scientific classification

1. Kingdom:	Animalia
2. Phylum:	Chordata
3. Subphylum:	Vertebrata
4. Class:	Reptilia
5. Order:	Squamata
6. Suborder:	Serpentes
7. Family:	Boidae
8. Genus:	Boa
9. Species:	B. constrictor

24. Boa constrictor is actually a generic name for various species of heavy-bodied snakes found in different parts of the world, ranging from tan to green in color.

25. All members of the Boidae family are constrictors, but only one species is referred to as boa constrictor: the red-tailed boa, which has tan-colored skin spotted with black blotches.

26. Boas are among the largest snakes in existence, ranging from 3 to 13 ft. long and weighing 22 to 33 lbs.

27. Female boas are generally larger than the males because of a phenomenon called sexual dimorphism.

28. Boas are nocturnal. It means they prefer to stay active during the night.

29. A boa constrictor's diet usually consists of small to average-sized rodents, although they are also reported to swallow larger prey such as ocelots (a big cat similar to jaguars and leopards).

30. Boas usually strike as a form of defense when they feel threatened. However, boas are not poisonous and their bites are rarely dangerous.

Figure 8: A green boa constrictor opens its mouth, ready to strike out at a potential threat. Because they are not poisonous, boas don't have fangs — but their bites will definitely hurt.

31.   Boas are one of the few snake species that give birth to their live young instead of laying eggs. The litter size varies from 10 to 65, with an average of 25 live young boas.

32.   Boas are captured and sold as exotic pets. Traders call them BCC, to distinguish them from another sub-species.

Cobra (Ophiophagus hannah)

Figure 9: The king cobra's hooded neck makes it unique from other types of snakes.

Scientific classification

1. Kingdom:	Animalia
2. Phylum:	Chordata
3. Subphylum:	Vertebrata
4. Class:	Reptilia
5. Order:	Squamata
6. Suborder:	Serpentes
7. Family:	Elapidae
8. Genus:	Ophiophagus
9. Species:	O. hannah

33.   Cobras are a large family of poisonous snakes, consisting about 270 species found around the world. However, the most famous variety known as the King Cobra does not share the same genus as most cobras.

34.   The king cobra is the largest and longest venomous snake in the world. A captive specimen has a recorded weight of 28 lbs. and a length of 14 ft. A specimen caught in the wild measured 16 ft. and weighed 26 lbs.

35.   A single bite from the King Cobra contains enough venom to kill an elephant.

Figure 10: Cobras are not confrontational by nature. Their first instinct is to flee from predators and other threats. However, they can become aggressive once they are provoked.

36.   King cobras are found mainly in India, Southeast Asia and East Asia. They are more active during the day than at night.

37.   Although highly dangerous, cobras usually flee from humans. They only strike when extremely provoked.

38.   Spitting cobras are a dangerous type of cobras that can eject venom from their fangs as a form of defense against predators.

39.   The king cobra varies in color from tan to black, with yellow cross-band markings all over its body.

40.   The king cobra's genus Ophiophagus derives its name from the Greek word for "snake-eater." This is because this snake's diet is mainly composed of other snakes, even venomous ones.

41.   The cobra's hiss has a much lower frequency than that of other snakes, that it is sometimes called a "growl."

42.   Female cobras hide their eggs in vegetation to incubate for 60 to 90 days (around 20 to 40 eggs per nest). They stay around to nest the eggs and defend them from potential predators.

43.   When the eggs hatch, the mother cobra leaves in search for prey to avoid eating her young.

Corn Snake (Pantherophis guttatus)

Figure 11: Corn snakes are a great help to farmers because they feed on the rodents that destroy the crops.

Scientific classification

1. Kingdom:	Animalia
2. Phylum:	Chordata
3. Subphylum:	Vertebrata
4. Class:	Reptilia
5. Order:	Squamata
6. Suborder:	Serpentes
7. Family:	Colubridae
8. Genus:	Pantherophis
9. Species:	P. guttatus

44.   Corn snakes, also called red rat snakes, are non-poisonous snakes that feed on mice and small rodents.

45.   Corn snakes are constrictors. It kills its prey by strangling it with its body.

46.   Corn snakes bear a physical resemblance to the venomous copperhead, but it is far more useful to humans. Corn snakes help control the population of rodent pests that infect and destroy farming crops.

Figure 12: Corn snakes are commonly found in Southeastern US states, while some sub-species are found in Mexico.

47.   The corn snake typically has brownish-red skin with orange saddles.

48.   Corn snakes are one of the few species which have been domesticated as pets.

49.   Before female corn snakes can breed, they need to undergo brumation, a cooling period that lasts 2 to 3 months. They must not be disturbed during this time.

50.   Corn snakes lay 12 to 24 eggs per mating season. Like most snake varieties, the corn snake abandons her eggs after laying them.

51.   Other than rodents, corn snakes are also known to feed on small lizards and amphibians.

Garter Snake (Thamnophis sirtalis)

Figure 13: Garter snakes get their name from the stripe markings on their bodies that make them resemble garters.

Scientific classification

1. Kingdom:	Animalia
2. Phylum:	Chordata
3. Subphylum:	Vertebrata
4. Class:	Reptilia
5. Order:	Squamata
6. Suborder:	Serpentes
7. Family:	Colubridae
8. Genus:	Thamnophis
9. Species:	T. sirtalis

52.   Garter snakes are one of the most common varieties of snakes found in North America, particularly in Canada and some parts of the US.

53.   Garter snakes are small and thin. On average, adult garter snakes reach only a length of 3 to 4 ft. long.

54.   Different species of garter snakes have different colors, but they have the same yellow stripe markings that make them look like garters. Common colors include black, brown, green, orange, and blue.

55.   Garter snakes are more active during the day. They are also known to bask under the sun during warmer climes.

Figure 14: Garter snakes hunt during the day and sleep at night in common dens with fellow garters. They eat anything they can overpower, including small rodents, birds, earthworms, and frogs.

56.   The saliva of garter snakes contains a mild toxin that affects only small reptiles and amphibians. For humans, the worst effect might be an allergic reaction (minor swelling and itching).

57.   One of the defense mechanisms of this snake is a foul-smelling liquid it releases when threatened.

58.   Male garter snakes pretend to be female garter snakes to lure their competition away from the real female. They can secrete false pheromones, the hormones that female snakes release when they are ready to mate.

59.   Baby snakes are born live from their mother's body. The eggs hatch inside her body.

60.   Garter snakes are one of the few species that have been domesticated by humans as pets.

Python (Pythonidae)

Figure 15: A python wraps itself around a tree branch. Trees and caves are among this snake's favorite habitats.

Scientific classification

1.	Kingdom:	Animalia
2.	Phylum:	Chordata
3.	Subphylum:	Vertebrata
4.	Class:	Reptilia
5.	Order:	Squamata
6.	Suborder:	Serpentes
7.	Family:	Pythonidae
8.	Genus:	Python
9.	Species:	P. regius

61. The python is a family of constrictor snakes that are found in tropical countries located near the equator.

62. There are a variety of python species, but the most famous python in the world today is the Python regius from Africa.

63. Python regius means "Royal python," because it is believed that Queen Cleopatra of Egypt wore this snake like a bracelet. It is also known as ball python because it curls into one when it is threatened.

64. The ball python is the smallest of its kind, with adults ranging only 3 to 4 ft. long. Only a few specimens have been recorded to have reached 5 to 6 ft. in length.

65. Pythons in general are one of the favorite snake pets because they have a docile temperament. Aside from ball pythons, Burmese pythons found in Southeast Asia are also often captured and sold as pets.

66.   Sadly, pythons are also often hunted and killed because of their beautiful skin pattern. Python skin is used to make bags, clothes, boots, and shoes.

67.   Female pythons lay eggs, ranging from 3 to 11 pieces at a time. Unlike most snakes which abandon their eggs, pythons nest their eggs to keep them warm and to guard against potential attackers.

68.   Pythons can be picky with what they eat, sometimes refusing to eat and hunt for weeks.

69.   Domestic breeders have now been able to produce pythons with different patterns and colors. Domesticated pythons are more docile than wild ones that have been captured.

Rattlesnake (Crotalinae)

Figure 16: A rattlesnake curls into a ball. The rattling sound that it makes comes from the rings on its tail whenever it moves.

Scientific classification

1. Kingdom:	Animalia
2. Phylum:	Chordata
3. Subphylum:	Vertebrata
4. Class:	Reptilia
5. Order:	Squamata
6. Suborder:	Serpentes
7. Family:	Viperidae
8. Subfamily:	Crotalinae

70.   Rattlesnakes are a sub-family of vipers also known as "pit vipers." Today, there are 32 identified species of rattlesnakes

found all over the US, Canada, Mexico, and some parts of South America.

71.   In addition to eyes, pit vipers like rattlesnakes also have a pair of pits that act like heat sensors. It helps them find their prey easily.

Figure 17: A rattlesnake is poised to defend itself from a threat. It moves its tail to produce the rattling sound to drive away potential predators.

72.   Rattlesnakes are named for the rattling sound they make when they move. This rattling sound is produced by the keratin rings found their tail.

73.   Rattlesnakes are poisonous. Their venom is hemotoxic, meaning it enters the prey's bloodstream and causes internal bleeding and pain. Some rattlesnakes can even paralyze their prey.

74.   The rings on the rattlesnake's tail are actually remnants of its old skin that remain after shedding. Each shedding adds a new ring to its tail.

75.   When treated immediately, rattlesnake bites on humans are not fatal, but it is the most frequent cause of snakebite injuries in the US.

76.   Rattlesnakes bite humans only when they are provoked or frightened. In fact, they are useful to farmers because they eat rodent pests that eat farm crops and spread diseases.

77.   Rattlesnakes don't lay eggs; they give birth to live young. They usually reproduce only on three year intervals.

Sea Snake (Hydrophiinae)

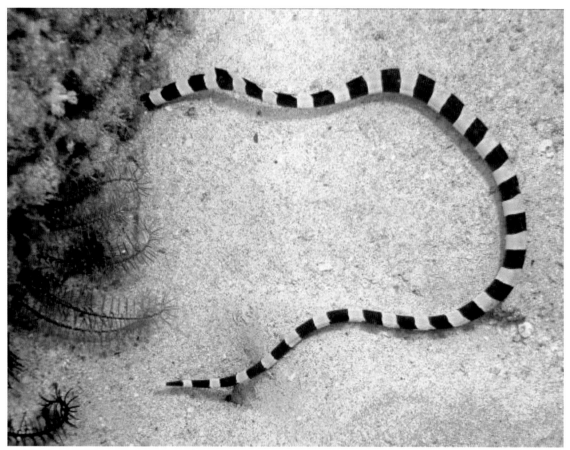

Figure 18: A sea snake crawls at the seabed in its search for prey. Sea snakes are marine creatures that live in the ocean during their entire lives.

Scientific classification

1. Kingdom:	Animalia
2. Phylum:	Chordata
3. Subphylum:	Vertebrata
4. Class:	Reptilia
5. Order:	Squamata
6. Suborder:	Serpentes
7. Family:	Elapidae
8. Subfamily:	Hydrophiinae

78.   Sea snakes are also called coral reef snakes. They are venomous marine reptiles that live in oceans and seas. Currently, there are 62 identified species that belong collectively to this group.

79.   The ancestors of modern sea snakes come from land, but they have adapted to life underwater. Most of them cannot move on land.

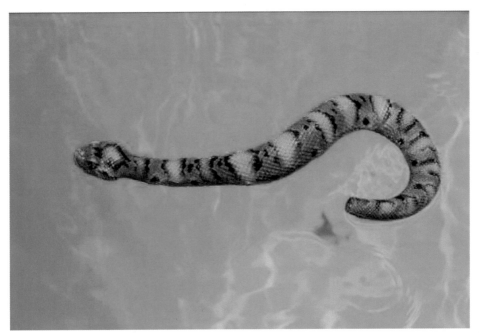

Figure 19: A sea snake coasts on the water surface to breathe air. It will dive under again to hunt for food and might not be back in the surface again for hours.

80.   Most sea snakes in the world are found in the Pacific and the Indian Ocean, often in warm shallow waters near the shoreline. There are no sea snakes in the Atlantic Ocean.

81.   Although they live in water for their entire lives, sea snakes still need air to breathe because they have lungs, not gills.

82. Sea snakes can stay underwater for several hours after surfacing to breathe because they also breathe through their skins.

83. Sea snakes are generally curious and gentle, but they become aggressive when provoked. They also tend to grow aggressive during their mating season.

84. Sea snakes are one of the most venomous varieties of snakes, but because they have short fangs, only a small amount of venom is injected to their targets. However, their bites could be fatal enough to paralyze and kill.

85. All but one genus of sea snakes give birth to live baby snakes. The sea kraits (Laticauda) are the only group of sea snakes that lay eggs on land.

86. Sea snakes eat small fish, mollusks, crustaceans, and eel found in shallow coral reefs and coastal waters.

87. Sea snakes are active on both day and night, unlike other terrestrial snakes that usually stay active only on one part of the day.

California King Snake (Lampropeltis getula californiae)

Figure 20: A California king snake basks under the sun. This snake is diurnal, which means it prefers to hunt at day instead of during the night.

Scientific classification

1. Kingdom:	Animalia
2. Phylum:	Chordata
3. Subphylum:	Vertebrata
4. Class:	Reptilia
5. Order:	Squamata
6. Suborder:	Serpentes
7. Family:	Colubridae
8. Genus:	Lampropeltis
9. Species:	L. getula californiae

88. The California king snake is a subspecies of king snakes found only in the West Coast of the US and some parts of Mexico. A captive specimen has escaped in Spain in 2007 and has been discovered to have adapted to the habitat there.

89. King snakes have been named as such because they also eat other snakes. The California king snake will eat a rattlesnake when given a chance.

90. California king snakes are average in length, reaching only around 4 ft. long in adulthood.

91. Aside from other snakes, the California kingsnake also eats rodents and birds, as well as small reptiles and amphibians.

92. Although non-poisonous, California king snakes easily overpower rattlesnakes by constriction. They are also immune to rattlesnake venom.

93. King snakes shed their skin about four to six times annually. Before every shedding, their eyes turn pale and their skin turns dull because of the dead skin they need to shed.

94. The California king snakes lay eggs, usually around 5 to 12 every time. They hatch after around 40 to 65 days.

Figure 21: California king snakes bred domestically have now morphed to different colors, skin markings and patterns. Pet king snakes should not be handled up to 48 hours after feeding them, because they might throw up their prey.

95.   California king snakes are a popular choice for snake owners because of their physical appearance. They can also be tamed and are easy to care for.

Milk Snake (Lampropeltis triangulum)

Figure 22: Milk snakes are a variety of king snakes that is found in the Americas, including the US, Canada, and South American countries like Ecuador and Venezuela.

Scientific classification

1. Kingdom:	Animalia
2. Phylum:	Chordata
3. Subphylum:	Vertebrata
4. Class:	Reptilia
5. Order:	Squamata
6. Suborder:	Serpentes
7. Family:	Colubridae
8. Genus:	Lampropeltis
9. Species:	L. triangulum

96.   A milk snake is a subspecies of king snakes that usually grow to the average length of 2 to 3 ft.

97.   Milk snakes are non-poisonous snakes that are often found in farmlands. They get their name from a popular belief that they drink milk from cows in the farms where they are found.

Figure 23: Milk snakes sometimes mimic the color of the poisonous coral snake to ward off predators.

98.   Milk snakes are often killed because they are mistaken as venomous coral snakes and rattlesnakes. They sometimes shake their tales very rapidly, causing to produce a sound similar to that of the rattlesnake's tail.

99.   Milk snakes are nocturnal. This means that they prefer to hunt at night and sleep by day.

100.   Milk snakes lay eggs instead of giving birth to live baby snakes. The female lays an average of 10 eggs per nest. The eggs take around 60 days to hatch.

101.   Milk snakes are also popularly bred domestically as pets. They are fed captive-bred mice and other rodents.

Made in the USA
Columbia, SC
22 August 2020